Using Circle Time for PHSE and Citizenship

teachers is an invaluable
'Citizenship National
's worth of circle time

ge and Viv Smith, the
including:

L initiative (Social and
w-up work are clearly
arning.
rence in the classroom
ersonal level, in their

nd headteacher. She is

orking as an Associate

Using Circle Time for PHSE and Citizenship

A year's plan for Key Stage 2 teachers

Daphne Gutteridge
and
Viv Smith

 Routledge
Taylor & Francis Group

LONDON AND NEW YORK

First published 2008 by Routledge
2 Park Square, Milton Park, Abingdon, Oxon, OX14 4RN

Simultaneously published in the USA and Canada
by Routledge
270 Madison Ave, New York, NY 10016

Routledge is an imprint of the Taylor & Francis Group, an informa business

© 2008 Daphne Gutteridge and Viv Smith

Typeset in Bembo by
Keystroke, 28 High Street, Tettenhall
Printed and bound in Great Britain by
TJ International Ltd, Padstow, Cornwall

British Library Cataloguing in Publication Data
A catalogue record for this book is available from the British Library

Library of Congress Cataloging in Publication Data
Gutteridge, Daphne, 1948–
   Using circle time for PHSE and citizenship : a year's plan for key stage 2
   teachers / Daphne Gutteridge and Viv Smith.
      p. cm.
   1. Early childhood education–Activity programs.   2. Citizenship–Study and teaching
   (Elementary)   I. Smith Viv, 1951–   II. Title.
   LB1139.35.A37G88 2008
   372.83′2–dc22   2007028588

ISBN10: 0–415–44592–2 (pbk)
ISBN10: 0–203–93278–1 (ebk)
ISBN13: 978–0–415–44592–4 (pbk)
ISBN13: 978–0–203–93278–0 (ebk)

Contents

Preface   vii

Introduction: Personal, Health and Social Education   **1**
The nature of PHSE   1
Circle time   1
Why is circle time so important?   2
The circle time session   3
Dos and don'ts for circle time   4

Section 1
Developing confidence and responsibility and making the
most of your abilities   **7**
1.1   The new school year   9
1.2   Self-esteem   10
1.3   Emotions: Anger   11
1.4   Emotions: Disappointment   13
1.5   Emotions: Excitement   15
1.6   Adult roles   17
1.7   School transfer   18
1.8   Handling money   20
1.9   Bereavement: Pets   21
1.10   Bereavement: Family   23

Section 2
Preparing to play an active role as citizens   **25**
2.1   Rules   27
2.2   Classroom rules   28
2.3   Rights and responsibilities   29
2.4   Democracy   30
2.5   Prejudice   31
2.6   Inequality   32
2.7   Diversity/respecting differences   33
2.8   Multiculturalism   34
2.9   Racism   35
2.10   The media   37

Section 3
Developing a healthy, safer lifestyle   **39**
3.1   Healthy eating   41
3.2   Taking risks   42

3.3	Keeping safe: Stranger danger	43
3.4	Keeping safe: Alcohol	44
3.5	Keeping safe: Smoking	45
3.6	Hygiene and health	46
3.7	Health and safety in school	47

Section 4
Developing good relationships and respecting the differences
between people   **49**

4.1	Friendship	51
4.2	Reconciliation within friendships	52
4.3	Resolving conflict	53
4.4	Bullying (1)	54
4.5	Bullying (2)	55
4.6	Disability	57
4.7	Gender/stereotyping	59
4.8	Families (1)	61
4.9	Families (2)	62
4.10	Families (3)	63

Section 5
Assessment, recording and reporting   **65**

Appendix
Useful resources for teachers   **75**

Preface

As two very experienced primary school teachers who shared a class of Year 4/5/6 pupils for over 10 years, we felt we wanted to share with primary colleagues some tried-and-tested ideas for delivering PHSE/Citizenship through circle time. We had used various resources ourselves but had not found a handbook of any kind which actually linked lessons systematically to the PHSE/Citizenship scheme of work, and that was aimed at Key Stage 2 pupils. We also wanted a straightforward approach in which a teacher could open the book and find a very user-friendly lesson plan that would enable them to conduct a circle time session at a moment's notice. They would have no need to search for additional resources or prepare worksheets, etc. This is what we have endeavoured to do with this book.

Delivering circle time in the way that we advocate in this text plays a huge part in equipping children with important life skills that are the essence of PHSE/Citizenship and underpins the new SEAL initiative (Social and Emotional Aspects of Learning) and ECM (Every Child Matters) agenda. We have seen, through our experience, how issues raised, listened to and discussed have impacted on children's ideas, thoughts and behaviours. Children find the sessions very stimulating and love the opportunity to be treated as adults, with their opinions sought and listened to.

Daphne Gutteridge and Viv Smith

Introduction: Personal, Health and Social Education

This book is designed to help teachers to plan and deliver the Personal, Health and Social Education (PHSE) and Citizenship curriculum for Key Stage 2 (KS2). The comprehensive coverage of the PHSE and Citizenship curriculum will develop pupils' skills, knowledge and understanding, including those linked to other curriculum areas.

The nature of PHSE

So much of this area of the curriculum is aimed at overall pupil personal development and well-being. This links very strongly with the Every Child Matters agenda and the SEAL initiative (Social and Emotional Aspects of Learning). All schools hope to develop mature, independent and self-confident pupils with an awareness and respect for others. **We strongly believe that this is the most important area of the whole curriculum and underpins all other work that takes place in the primary school classroom.** Working through photocopiable worksheets is often used as an easy way to deliver this area of the curriculum, and a wealth of printed resources have appeared on the market to meet this need. However, we feel that this is not the most effective way to work with pupils and to develop their thinking. The most effective tool to deliver many of the skills, knowledge and understanding is through circle time.

It is vital that teachers are sensitive to their own school ethos and situation, but we hope that the ideas presented here for teachers will be helpful in planning and delivering circle time with their own class of KS2 pupils. The sessions can be used with all of KS2, but teachers may feel that some lessons need to be adapted to suit the level of maturity of their own class.

Circle time

Over time, we want pupils to develop their own opinions and ideas and be able to express themselves with confidence. We develop our ideas by listening to the views of other people and through discussion. This interaction with others in a meaningful context develops pupils' thinking and problem-solving skills. Circle time provides an ideal vehicle for this in school and, when used as a regular activity in class, encourages high level discussion across a wide range of issues, including some very sensitive subjects.

The setting of the session is important and it should be held in the classroom if possible. This is the pupils' own familiar space and the circle works best here. This has implications for timing as it is often necessary to rearrange furniture before the session. Groups of pupils can be given responsibility for setting up the room in readiness. The authors found that the session directly after lunch worked well. Three or four pupils rearrange the classroom during the lunchtime. The teacher planned a following lesson that could be delivered in the circle, for example Music, or the class all worked together co-operatively at the end of the session to return the room to normal.

We must reiterate here that circle time must be held regularly every week in order to be most effective in promoting and developing pupils' skills. Each session will last approximately 20 minutes.

Teachers will need to adjust the material in relation to their own classes and age groups. For example, Year 6 pupils may be able to discuss issues in greater depth and at a high level, whereas Year 3 pupils will be working at a much simpler level.

Layout and approach

Many aspects of PHSE and Citizenship in your school will be delivered in other areas of the curriculum. Cross-curricular links, including ECM (Every Child Matters) and the SEAL initiative (Social and Emotional Aspects of Learning) can be found at the end of each lesson plan.

Plans and resources for topics that can be most effectively addressed through circle time are presented as units of work to aid teachers in their planning. Assessment ideas, recording templates and additional resources appear at the end of the book.

Why is circle time so important?

Delivering circle time in the way that we advocate in this text plays a huge part in equipping children with important life skills. We have seen, through our experience, how issues raised, listened to and discussed have impacted on children's ideas, thoughts and behaviours. There are many positive reasons for making circle time a regular feature in your class:

- There is no right or wrong answer – all contributions are valued

- It develops maturity and self-confidence

- It develops awareness of and respect for others (including the teacher/teaching assistant/pupil support worker)

- The class bonds as a unit

- It develops speaking and listening skills

- It develops pupil self-esteem

- It enables children to make discoveries about others (including their peers/teacher/other adults)

- Less able pupils are given an equal voice

- It develops their own thinking

- They develop confidence in expressing their own opinions

- It helps pupils solve problems/deal with conflicts

- It helps pupils to realise that inequalities exist in society.

We recognise that teachers may have some worries, including:

- Apprehension about trying out a session as you need to relinquish some control – the pupils drive the discussion and you have to 'go with the flow'

- It is important to not be judgemental – teachers need to accept all contributions without negative comment – and some may find this difficult

- Both teachers and pupils may feel under pressure to speak
- The teacher needs to be honest in sharing their thoughts and feelings and be prepared to 'bare their soul'
- Teachers may feel concern about handling any sensitive issues that may arise
- There may be difficulties in setting up the classroom, e.g. rearranging furniture
- Finding time for the session (approximately 20 minutes) in the busy primary school day
- Planning for the sessions may be seen as a burden.

We do appreciate that teachers may feel apprehensive about conducting a circle time for the first time, but be confident and 'have a go'. Regular circle times develop a positive ethos in the classroom in which children are listened to and in which they listen to each other.

The circle time session

Circle time follows a set format including certain elements in each session. Twenty minutes each week should be set aside for a regular Circle, although when the children become very animated and involved in a discussion, it could last much longer! If the teacher feels that it is beneficial to continue the discussion with the class, we would urge that they do so (depending on their situation/curriculum constraints).

The elements to include in your lesson are as follows.

1. Reiterate rules

It is important to invite one pupil to remind the class of the rules before every session. There are two basic rules:

a)   Don't speak when someone else is speaking

b)   Respect everything anyone says.

Initially, it may be necessary to explain what is meant by respecting contributions, (e.g. not laughing at anyone) and explain that what is said in the circle is confidential, and what this means.

2. Silent statements

Pupils are invited to change places, without speaking, in response to introductory statements from the teacher. In this way, all pupils are making a statement about themselves or their feelings without using words. The teacher and any adults involved will also change places in response. The statements will usually be related to the theme of the circle time session. (Refer to individual lessons plans for suggestions of silent statements.)

3. Question round

At this point, the teacher may wish to share the theme and learning objective for the circle time.
The teacher will ask one or two questions, which are passed around the circle, and everyone is invited to answer. Again, the questions will be based on the theme of the session. Children are allowed to pass, but should know that the teacher will return and offer them an opportunity to express their opinion at the end. The pupil may still pass. Some children may pass for several sessions at first; some may begin by copying answers given by others. This is perfectly acceptable

as they soon develop confidence to offer their own opinions. It is an opportunity for all children to have the chance to speak and be listened to.

4. Open discussion

The discussion is developed by inviting further ideas and opinions from anyone who wishes to contribute further through a show of hands. Follow-up questions may be used, or points raised in the previous round picked up and developed by the teacher.

5. Conclusion

This section acts like a plenary, when the ideas and themes of the circle are reiterated or summed up for everyone or the learning objective is revisited. It may take various forms:

- ideas may be recorded for classroom display

- any action decided on to be recorded/agreed by everyone

- a suitable poem may be used to reinforce the theme visited

- the teacher may think that a time of quiet reflection could be appropriate at this point (these are marked in the text)

- occasionally, pupils may be invited to vote on the issues raised. The teacher always needs to give the pupils a few moments to think through their response beforehand. The authors found through experience that, when invited to vote, some pupils may be influenced by friends or others in class, but reminding them each time to give their own opinion and not to be influenced by others gradually develops their confidence to make up their own minds and express their own thoughts.

Dos and don'ts for circle time

We have developed a useful checklist of dos and don'ts that we have found make circle time successful for teachers and children.

Dos and don'ts checklist for circle times

Do:
- ✓ Recap on the rules for the Circle each session.
- ✓ Ensure everyone is in place and seated in the circle ready to begin. Make it different to other lessons.
- ✓ Hold regular circle times – at least 20 minutes every week.
- ✓ Accept all contributions without appearing judgemental in any way.
- ✓ Allow pupils to pass, but let them know that you'll return and offer them a second chance to contribute at the end.
- ✓ Accept that children may initially copy others' contributions – they'll stop this as they gain confidence.

Don't:
- ✗ Be afraid to have a go!
- ✗ Be critical of children's responses. If a comment is made that you feel is inappropriate, throw the discussion open for all to comment.
- ✗ Let any one child dominate the discussion.
- ✗ Give up if your first circle time is not successful.
- ✗ Mention individuals by name, unless it is to make a positive comment about them, e.g. 'Ann was very kind to me today.'
- ✗ Abandon the session half way through.
- ✗ Exclude any pupil if at all possible.

Do:

✓ Have a plan and stick to the agenda.

✓ Conclude every session on a positive note.

✓ Encourage everyone to participate in open discussion.

✓ Be prepared to contribute along with the children.

Section I

Developing confidence and responsibility and making the most of your abilities

The themes and topics in this section are linked to Section 1 of the PHSE/Citizenship scheme of work:

- The new school year

- Self-esteem

- Emotions: Anger

- Emotions: Disappointment

- Emotions: Excitement

- Adult roles

- School transfer

- Handling money

- Bereavement: Pets

- Bereavement: Family

Theme 1.1 The new school year

This session can be used at the beginning of the new school year to enable the class to get to know their new teacher or the new mix of children in a mixed-age group situation.

Links

- PHSE/Cit: Unit 1a, 1c, 2d
- SEAL: New Beginnings, Changes
- ECM: Enjoy and Achieve

Learning objective

To ensure that everyone feels comfortable and positive about the new school year.

Reiterate rules

Ask one of the pupils to remind everyone of the circle time rules.

Silent statements

Change places if you were looking forward to coming back to school.

Change places if you were not looking forward to coming back to school.

Question round

What aspects of school were you looking forward to?

What things were you not sure/worried about?

Open discussion

What makes the classroom a happy place in which to be?

The teacher at this point needs to pick up on any issues raised in the question round – particularly any worries they have identified. Ask if the group can make any suggestions to make people feel better/allay any worries or fears.

Conclusion

Invite the group to formulate a statement for the class:

'We want our class to be..........'

Record and display this in the classroom.

Theme 1.2 Self-esteem

Learning objective

To encourage everyone to feel positive about themselves and increase their self-esteem.

Reiterate rules

Ask one of the pupils to remind everyone of the circle time rules.

Links

- PHSE/Cit: Unit 1a, 1b
- SEAL: Good to be me
- ECM: Be Healthy
- Literacy: Use Harry Potter text for character study work
- Music: Use M People track – 'What Have You Done Today To Make You Feel Proud?'

Silent statements

Change places if you have done anything this week that you have felt proud about. Change places if you have been praised this week by an adult (teacher, parent, etc.).

Question round

Tell us something about yourself – something you think is one of your good points.

Turn to the person on your right and tell us all something you think they are good at (in or out of school) or something that you like about them.

(In both of these rounds, the children can use abilities or qualities.)

Open discussion

Can anyone explain how it feels when someone praises you?

Do you think it is important to be praised when you've done something well?

Why?

How would it affect you if no-one ever praised your efforts?

(The teacher could bring Harry Potter's treatment by the Dursleys into the conversation.)

Conclusion

Reflect on how you feel when you've done something well while you listen to the M People song 'What Have You Done Today To Make You Feel Proud?'

Give the children a challenge to praise someone during the coming week.

The teacher can display a notice on the wall to remind everyone:

'Have you praised anyone today?'

(Take feedback from this notice at the beginning of the next circle time.)

Theme 1.3 Emotions: Anger

It is very important for the teacher and any adults in the circle to participate and share their emotions honestly with the children. Children don't always think of their teachers as people who can also be upset or angry when treated badly.

Learning objective

To help everyone recognise that anger is a destructive emotion and that they need to develop strategies to deal with angry feelings.

Reiterate rules

Ask one of the pupils to remind everyone of the circle time rules.

Silent statement

Change places if you have felt angry with someone this week.

Question round

Change places if someone has been angry with you this week.

How do you feel when someone is angry with you?

How do you feel when you are angry?

(*Talk about expressions for anger, e.g. seeing red – can they understand why people use this expression?*)

Read the poem overleaf and answer the questions.

Open discussion

What kind of things make you really angry?

The teacher needs to pick up on children's ideas and ask the group for appropriate ways to deal with particular situations. Children can also suggest inappropriate ways. How do inappropriate responses make things worse?

Conclusion

Reflect on how best to deal with negative feelings. It may be helpful to play some peaceful music during the reflection time. Record some of the strategies for dealing with angry feelings suggested by the children in some way – maybe a book of scenarios and appropriate responses.

Links

- PHSE/Cit: Unit 1a, 1d
- SEAL: Getting On and Falling Out
- ECM: Be Healthy
- Literacy: write own poems to be displayed with art work
- Science: This could form part of the science unit dealing with mood swings during puberty
- Art/Music: Pupils can listen to 'Mars' from the *Planet Suite*. Discuss the emotions suggested by the music. Discuss colours associated with the emotion. Look at some abstract work by Jackson Pollock. Pupils can then produce their own abstract to represent anger

Anger

All was blue skies
When suddenly the black cloud appeared
And dropped its acid rain,
Penetrating my brain
And exploding inside.
My eyes turned to blood
And my mouth spat out grotesque words
That no-one understood.

Jagged fragments hurtled south
'Til my chest heaved
And my hands scattered like leaves
On a hurricane day.
My legs jerked as if possessed
By an ugly force
Taking its course through my body.

And then it was gone
As quickly as it came
And I became
Weak, puzzled
And
Alone.

Viv Smith

What might have made the poet be so angry?

Why do you think the last word of the poem is 'alone'?

Theme 1.4 Emotions: Disappointment

Learning objective

To develop understanding that everyone experiences disappointment in their lives but that we need to move on from it.

Reiterate rules

Ask one of the pupils to remind everyone of the circle time rules.

Silent statement

Today we are going to put everyone's name in a hat and draw out four names and offer them a treat. Change places if you would be disappointed not to be chosen.

Question round

How do you feel when you are disappointed about something?
Can you tell us about an occasion when you felt really disappointed about something?

Open discussion

(It is often very useful to give the children a scenario to discuss that they may experience at some time and work through appropriate strategies for dealing with the situation.)

You have been invited to your best friend's party. Nearly all of the class will be there. Your parents/carers will not allow you to go because you have to go to visit Granny. How do you feel? What do you do? How can you resolve the problem?

Discuss the word compromise and explain what it means – maybe they will allow you and your friend a treat or take you both out for a burger, etc.

You may wish to share the poem 'Disappointment', which appears overleaf.

Conclusion

Choose the four names from the hat. They get to choose a treat for the rest of the class – maybe five minutes of extra playtime, a game for the last five minutes of the day or biscuits for everyone at snack time. How do you feel now? All things usually work out in the end and sometimes disappointments are sorted.

Links

- PHSE/Cit: Unit 1a, 1d
- SEAL: Good to be me
- ECM: Be Healthy
- Literacy: Writing own short playscript based on the theme
- RE/Assembly: The Story of Esau and Jacob from Genesis Chapter 25

Disappointment

We were united
All excited
Then it was decided
Now we're divided

Down to four
I stare at the floor,
Don't want to be ignored.
Down to four.

Please let it be me,
Now there's only three.
I'm the best, anyone would agree.
Please let it be me.

Now there's just two . . .
Please don't let it be you
I've just got to get through
Please don't let it be you.

I got right to the end,
But it's happened again.
They've chosen my friend.
I've got right to the end!

Not selected –
Been rejected.
Feel dejected.
Life's an elective.

Viv Smith

What do you think was being decided upon in this poem?

What do you think the last line means?

Theme 1.5 Emotions: Excitement

Learning objective

To help everyone understand that excitement is a positive emotion but that we need to contain it sensibly.

Reiterate rules

Ask one of the pupils to remind everyone of the circle time rules.

Silent statements

Change places if you have any occasion coming soon that you are excited about.

Change places if you feel excited about .... *you can use any occasion relevant at the time, e.g. the school play, our class trip, sports day, etc.*

Question round

How do you feel when you are excited about something?

Can you tell us about an occasion when you felt really excited about something that was going to happen?

Open discussion

Do your parents/teachers ever get cross with you when you are excited? Why do you think this is? Have you ever felt cross with a friend when they are excited about something? Why?

Conclusion

It is often useful to use a relevant poem as a basis for discussion or as a conclusion to recap on the discussion.

Share the poem 'Excitement' with the class, then ask the follow-up questions.

Emotion is a very important topic to address with the class. Other emotions are dealt with in this book:

Jealousy – See Relationships (Section 4: Theme 10)

Sadness and grief – See Bereavement (Section 1: Themes 9 and 10)

Hurt/anger – See Relationships (Section 4: Themes 2 and 3)

Links

- PHSE/Cit: Unit 1a, 1d
- SEAL: Good to be me
- ECM: Be Healthy
- Dance: Use Excitement as a theme – music suggestions 'I Feel Excited' by The Pointer Sisters or the theme from *Fame* by Irene Cara
- Art: Having listened to the music, pupils could look at Mondrian's work and create their own pieces using bright colours but contained within geometric shapes

Excitement

Three days to go
I can feel the glow
Spreading through me,
Until it reaches my face
And a smile as wide as space
Appears from nowhere.

Two days to go
And though
I try to hide that smile
It won't budge.
But no-one can see
The warm waves inside of me.
Or hear the sound of glee
In my ears.

One day to go
Time's so slow
But I can't keep the laughter in,
Or the grin
Playing on my lips.
I'm in the mood for fun
And I run in meaningless circles.

Here at last!
But now time moves so fast.
I need to remember each bit of it.
What's been the best?
The feeling of complete happiness.

Viv Smith

Why do you think the poet was excited? What was she waiting for?

Have you ever felt like this or done any of these things when you have been excited?

Theme 1.6 Adult roles

This template could form the basis of a series of circle times in which the teacher invites a number of visitors to the circle for the children to talk to. A list of possible visitors is included at the end of the lesson plan.

Learning objective

To develop respect for other people's work/career choices and raise awareness of different working roles.

Reiterate rules

Ask one of the pupils to remind everyone of the circle time rules. Then, introduce the session by asking children what different jobs for adults are there in school?

Silent statements

Change places if your parent/carer has a job outside the home.

Change places if you have ever been to work with them.

Question round

What job would you like to do when you leave school and why?

Open discussion

The teacher will introduce the visitor. They will be invited to briefly describe their job. Children can then ask them questions about their job and why they chose to do it.

Conclusion

The teacher can ask the visitor what they would say was the best thing and the worse thing about their job.

Children can then think about this and take a vote – Who would like to carry out this job? Who would not? Who isn't sure and abstains? (Explain abstension.)

Possible visitors for this series of circle times

Headteacher, teacher, teaching assistant, secretary, cook, caretaker, governor, dinner lady, traffic patrol, nurse, EWO. Visitors from outside of school can be included – choose a good cross-section – electrician, chef, shop assistant, car mechanic, local bank worker, post office clerk, librarian, parent with interesting job, etc.

Links

- PHSE/Cit: Unit 1a, 1e
- SEAL: Going for Goals
- ECM: Enjoy and Achieve/Achieve Economic Well-being
- Literacy: Write what they have learned from the visitor in interview format
- ICT: Research different jobs on the internet

Theme 1.7 School transfer

Learning objective

To prepare pupils for transfer to secondary school (Year 6 pupils).

Reiterate rules

Ask one of the pupils to remind everyone of the circle time rules.

Silent statements

Change places if you are looking forward to going to your new school.

Change places if you have any worries about moving on to your new school.

Question round

Tell us some of the things you are looking forward to in your new school.

What worries do you have about moving to secondary school?

Open discussion

Present some scenarios dealing with some of the issues that children may identify as a worry, for example:

1) You miss the bus home – what could you do?

   a)   Make your own way home.

   b)   Go back and tell someone in school what has happened.

   c)   Use your mobile phone to ring home.

   d)   Go home with a friend.

Discuss each option and why (b) is a better solution than (a) or (d).

2) You have no-one to play with at lunchtime – what do you do?

   a)   Just hang around on your own.

   b)   Try and find someone in your class and talk to them.

   c)   Look for someone else on their own and talk to them.

   d)   Ask if you can go inside and read.

Links

- PHSE/Cit: Unit 1a, 1b, 1c
- SEAL: New Beginnings Changes
- ECM: Enjoy and Achieve/Make a Positive Contribution
- Literacy: Produce their own pamphlet with hints and tips for smooth transfer

Discuss each option as above and agree on the best solution.

3) Your bag has gone missing and you think someone may have hidden it – what would you do?

    a) Tell the teacher.

    b) Tackle the suspect.

    c) Discuss what to do with a friend.

    d) Ignore it and hope it will be returned.

Again, discuss each option as above and agree on the best solution.

Conclusion

Reflect on all the things that you are going to enjoy in your new school. You could play 'Changes' by Ozzie and Kelly Osbourne at this point.

Tell the children that you will leave a box in the classroom. They can write any worries they may have and wish to discuss on a slip of paper (anonymously if they wish). These can be picked up and dealt with in a further circle time. Alternatively, the teacher could display these worries and pupils could be invited to write up coping strategies that can be shared with class and form the basis of further discussion.

Note: Teachers can devise similar scenarios to use with their class. A range of such scenarios are available in a transfer game 'Moving On' produced by the Lancashire Healthy Schools team (www.lancsngfl.ac.uk).

Theme 1.8 Handling money

Learning objective

To develop an understanding of how best to look after money and realise the value of saving.

(**Note**: The teacher will need to prepare a form – see conclusion.)

Reiterate rules

Ask one of the pupils to remind everyone of the circle time rules.

Silent statements

Change places if you get a set amount of pocket money each week.

Change places if you are given money when you ask for it.

Change places if you do jobs at home to earn money.

Question round

Have you ever saved up for something expensive that you really wanted? If so, what was it? How long did you save?

Have you ever been told by your parents that you have to wait for something expensive that you really wanted? If so, what was it and how long did you have to wait?

Open discussion

Do you think it is a good idea to get regular pocket money? Why/why not? How much do you think is a realistic amount of money for you to get? Does anybody have any good ideas about how and where to save your money?

Conclusion

The teacher should obtain or devise a form to apply to open a savings account at the bank. Children can try filling in the form.

Note: A follow-up circle time can be held with an advisor from the local bank to discuss savings accounts and how they work.

Links

- PHSE/Cit: Unit 1f
- SEAL: Going for Goals
- ECM: Achieve Economic Well-Being
- Literacy: Link to formal letter writing – write to a bank to request information or arrange for a visit
- Maths: Calculating the amount that could be saved over various periods of time
- ICT: Link to a unit on spreadsheets and use the spreadsheet to carry out calculations

Theme 1.9 Bereavement: Pets

Learning objective

To understand more about changes that take place in our lives.

Reiterate rules

Ask one of the pupils to remind everyone of the circle time rules.

Silent statements

Change places if you have a pet.

Change places if you have had a pet that died.

Question round

Why do you think that many people have pets?

Are there any drawbacks to owning a pet?

(Possible responses – time consuming, cost, responsibility, cruel if you are at work all day, they can be destructive, the pet may die.)

Open discussion

Would anyone like to share with the circle about a pet they have loved and lost (or the family has lost)?

Is this a good reason not to have a pet?

(The teacher needs to steer the discussion in positive way – so much enjoyment and fun and that memories of the pet are precious to have.)

Conclusion

The children can be invited to bring in pictures of both past/present pets to share with the class – a possible display idea.

Share the poem overleaf.

Links

- PHSE/Cit: Unit1a, 1d
- SEAL: Changes
- ECM: Make a Positive Contribution
- Literacy: Write own leaflet on looking after pets
- ICT: Internet research on looking after pets

Sometimes . . .

Sometimes,
When I close my eyes,
I can see you running towards me.
Sometimes,
When I listen extra hard,
I can hear you greeting me as I fling open the door.
Sometimes,
If I really sniff the air, I can smell your warm coat.
Sometimes,
If I stay very still, I can feel your breath hot on my legs
And your soft fur brushing through my fingers.
Sometimes,
In the kitchen, I imagine your bowl filled with food
And your basket with the cosy rug.
Sometimes,
When I wake, I think your rough tongue is licking my face
And your cold nose is nuzzling under the covers.
Sometimes,
Just as I sleep, I taste the tears
And remember the pain inside my chest
When I whisper your name.

Viv Smith

Theme 1.10 Bereavement: Family

This is obviously a very sensitive area, but if used appropriately can help pupils to deal with their feelings. This circle time can be adapted and used when national incidents in the news cause children to ask questions, for example about a natural disaster causing death or the death of someone in the public eye.

Links

- PSHE/Cit: Unit 1a, 1d
- SEAL: Changes
- ECM: Make a Positive Contribution

Learning objective

To understand more about the changes that take place in our life.

Reiterate rules

Ask one of the pupils to remind everyone of the circle time rules.

Question round

Can you tell us what kind of things you enjoy doing with your grandparents?

Does anyone have a special memory of a particular time that you spent with a grandparent – what happened and what did you do?

Share a story with the circle

(The teacher can choose one of the stories listed below to use with the children – all deal sensitively with bereavement.)

Open discussion

We all know that everyone cannot live forever. Would anyone like to tell us about a friend or relative that has died?

If the teacher feels able, they could begin by sharing one of their experiences with the children.

Conclusion

Reflection: Think about anyone who is special to you.

What do you think is the best way to celebrate the life of someone we've lost?

(Remember times spent with them, look at photos, look at presents given, etc.)

The teacher could play 'Father and Son' by Cat Stevens during reflection.

If appropriate for the class/age group, the class could produce a 'Special People in our Lives' book. The following books may be useful for teachers to use with their pupils when dealing with the sensitive subject of bereavement:

Grandpa	John Burningham
	(This is a picture book and could be used with younger pupils.)
Beautiful	Susi Fowler
Michael Rosen's Sad Book	Michael Rosen
Vicky Angel	Jacqueline Wilson

Section 2

Preparing to play an active role as citizens

Themes and topics explored in this section are linked to Section 2 of the PHSE/Citizenship scheme of work:

- Rules

- Classroom rules

- Rights and responsibilities

- Democracy

- Prejudice

- Inequality

- Diversity/respecting differences

- Multiculturalism

- Racism

- The media

Theme 2.1 Rules

Learning objectives

To develop an understanding that groups/communities/society need rules to function successfully.

Reiterate rules

Ask one of the pupils to remind everyone of the circle time rules.

Silent statements

Change places only if you are a boy and your name begins with S.

Change places only if you are a girl and your hair is long.

Teachers can use any variations of the above statements, and add more in a similar vein.

Question round

Think about any rules you may have in your house. Can you share one of your rules from home with everyone?

Open discussion

Do you think it's a good idea to have rules? Why? What would it be like if there were no rules? What happens if you break a rule?

Establish through discussion that communities need rules to be happy and successful and to function well.

The teacher could read an extract from *Matilda* by Roald Dahl to explore how life might be without rules and what effect this may have on an individual.

Conclusion

Recap on what has been said about the importance of rules. For next time, be thinking of some rules that you think would be very important for our classroom.

Pin a sheet to the wall so that children can write up their suggestions.

Links

- PHSE/Cit: Unit 1a, 2b
- SEAL: Getting On and Falling Out
- ECM: Make a Positive Contribution
- Literacy: Writing instruction texts – rules for games
- Develop work from *Matilda* by Roald Dahl as a basis for writing. They could describe life without rules or use as a stimulus for letter writing – Matilda writing to a friend, describing her life and how she would like it to be different
- RE/Assembly: The Ten Commandments, Exodus Chapter 20
- PE: Establishing the importance of safety rules and rules in games

Theme 2.2 Classroom rules

Learning objectives

To give everyone joint responsibility for their class rules.

Reiterate rules

Ask one of the pupils to remind everyone of the circle time rules.

Silent statements

Sometimes, a game can be played at this stage. This game can be played as children are following rules for changing places.

Children can be given the name of an item of stationery – pencil, pen, ruler, eraser – around the circle. Then pens can change place with erasers, pencils with rulers, etc. When the teacher says 'pencil case', everyone changes places.

Question round

Think about any rules that you may have in your house.

Have you broken any this week? Which one? What was the result?

Open discussion

Share the rules that the children wrote up on the sheet following the previous circle time. Do the children want to add any additional ones?

If you have helped to set the rules, do you think it's more likely that you will keep them? Why?

Discuss how many rules we need for the class – we need important ones only.

We found from experience that four or five were enough. The following rules were those usually suggested by the children and which everyone was happy with:

a)   Be a good listener.

b)   Treat others as you would wish them to treat you.

c)   Respect our classroom and our resources.

d)   Work together and create a peaceful working environment.

The teacher will need to lead the discussion and consolidate the children's suggestions – some can be joined to make one rule, some duplicate what they want to say – but give everyone a hearing.

Conclusion

The teacher should present six or seven rules and get the children to vote for the four or five rules that they think are most important and want for their class. Display these rules in the classroom so that they can easily be referred to as and when necessary.

Links

- PHSE/Cit: Unit 1a, 2b
- SEAL: New Beginnings
- ECM: Make a Positive Contribution
- ICT: Children can present the rules they agree on for display. Children may also print a copy of the rules for themselves, which could be pasted into their planner or one of their exercise books

Theme 2.3 Rights and responsibilities

Learning objective

To raise awareness of everyone's rights, but to understand that everyone has responsibilities too.

(**Note**: teachers will need a copy of the United Nations Children's Charter, available from www.childrens-charterofrights.com/poster1.)

Reiterate rules

Ask one of the pupils to remind everyone of the circle time rules.

Silent statements

If you're allowed to visit a friend's house unaccompanied, change places.

If you're allowed to ride your bike on the road, change places.

If you're allowed to make a cup of tea on your own, change places.

Question round

Are you responsible for anything in particular at home – if so what?

(Examples may include cleaning your own room, looking after a younger sibling or a pet, loading the dishwasher, etc.)

Open discussion

What does 'having rights' mean?

Do you think you have any rights as a child?

(Children should suggest a right to food, shelter, education, clothing, a safe environment, etc.)

Teachers can display the United Nations Children's Charter (see Appendix).

Do you think this applies to all children? Has it always been so?

The teacher can read an extract from *Oliver Twist* by Charles Dickens, *The Water Babies* by Charles Kingsley or *The Street Child* by Berlie Doherty.

Because we all have rights, we also all have responsibilities – what do you think they may be?

(Children should suggest obeying parents/teachers, respecting society's rules, looking after possessions, keeping clean/healthy, always doing one's best, etc.)

Conclusion

Ask the children if they think it would be a good idea to display the United Nation's Charter in the classroom for them to read and think about at leisure. Identify together a responsibility that corresponds to each point on the charter.

Links

- PHSE/Cit: Unit 1a, 2d
- SEAL: Relationships
- ECM: Stay Safe
- ICT: Use the Internet for history research on children in the past
- History: Link to the history study units on the Victorians or the Tudors

Theme 2.4 Democracy

Learning objective

That everyone should understand what democracy means and why we have elections.

Reiterate rules

Ask one of the pupils to remind everyone of the circle time rules.

Silent statements

Change places if you enjoy working with a group.

Change places if you prefer to work alone.

Question round

What do you think is good about working in a group?

Why do you think that teachers sometimes put you in groups to work?

What problems arise when you work in a group?

Open discussion

Imagine that the teacher has put you into groups and has asked each group to choose an animal to research and give a presentation to the rest of the class. How would you go about deciding which animal to research?

Imagine that the teacher has told the class that they could choose a treat for good work. How would the class go about choosing a treat that would be acceptable to everyone?

The teacher needs to bring out in the discussion that everyone has to have a voice, but in the end a decision has to be made that may not be always acceptable to everyone, but pleases the majority. Here, the teacher can introduce the word 'democracy' and explain what it means.

Conclusion

If it has been a successful circle time, the teacher could allow the children to decide on a treat by democratic means (this may be reached by discussion or by voting). This topic is quite complicated and children can find it difficult to understand. It is much more meaningful therefore to work through the whole process with the class so they experience it.

This topic could be delivered during a history topic on Ancient Greece or addressed during national or local elections. It is effective to run a class election to help children understand the roles and the process, so children should form different parties and formulate their policies. Candidates can then make a pitch to the rest of the class followed by a secret ballot. Returning officer can then count votes and announce the result. Many schools now have a School Council and it can also be related to these elections.

Useful web sites for teachers:

www.localdemocracy.org.uk   www.dfes.gov.uk/citizenship
www.bys.org.uk   www.mockelections.co.uk
www.teachingcitizenship.org.uk

The authors found the Channel 4 DVD *The X File* a useful resource in helping children to understand democracy.

Links

- PHSE/Cit: Unit 1a, 2a, 2g
- SEAL: Relationships/Getting On and Falling Out; Formation of a School Council (see www.schoolcouncils.org)
- ECM: Make a Positive Contribution
- History: Link to the study unit on the Ancient Greeks (the earliest record of voting; see also Democracy 2)

Theme 2.5 Prejudice

This can be a very difficult topic to deal with in some school situations and teachers need to be sensitive when handling the issues raised here.

Learning objective

That everyone should understand what the terms 'prejudice' and 'equal opportunity' mean and to recognise that inequality still exists in society.

Reiterate rules

Ask one of the pupils to remind everyone of the circle time rules.

Silent statements

Change places if you know someone who lives in another country.

Change places if you know someone who speaks another language.

Change places if you know someone who follows a different religion.

Question round

Is there anything that you feel you can't do because you are a girl/boy – what?

Open discussion

Does anyone know what the term prejudice means? (Explain so that they all understand – prejudice is when people are treated unfairly just because they are different in some way.)
Who do you think may experience prejudice in our society?

(The following groups should be mentioned: religious, ethnic, gender, disabilities, overweight people, old people. Some school groups may mention people who are gay – the teacher should accept this along with other contributions.)

Has anyone ever heard of Anne Frank?
The teacher can give a short explanation of who she was and what happened to her. A short extract from the book could be read to the class.

Why do you think that this particular group experiences prejudice?

Establish through discussion that ignorance is the root of most prejudice, which is why learning about others, their feelings and their beliefs is so important.
How do you think society tries to overcome prejudice?

Conclusion

Further extracts from *The Diary of Anne Frank* (or from any of the alternative texts mentioned above) could be read or, if the teacher can obtain the video of the story, that may be used.

Links

- PHSE/Cit: Unit 4b, 4d, 4e, 4f
- SEAL: Relationships/Getting On and Falling Out
- ECM: Make a Positive Contribution
- Literacy: *The Diary of Anne Frank*, *Rose Blanche* by Roberto Innocenti or *Coming Home* by Floella Benjamin may be used as a basis for their own writing about emotions. (The Floella Benjamin text would be more suitable for younger pupils.)
- History: Link to the unit of work on Britain since the 1930s, covering World War 2 and the Holocaust
- RE: Unit 4D Religions represented in our Neighbourhood

Theme 2.6 Inequality

Learning objective

To be aware that many inequalities exist in the world.

Reiterate rules

Ask one of the pupils to remind everyone of the circle time roles.

Silent statements

Change places if you have ever given money to a charity.

Change places if you have ever watched an item on the news or seen a TV programme showing how people in another country are experiencing hardship.

Question round

How did it make you feel when you watched these programmes?

Open discussion

The open discussion should be based on the materials chosen by the teacher from the resources suggested produced by Christian Aid.

Conclusion

The children are usually very interested and often shocked at how some children have to live, often prompting a wish to undertake fundraising events. This could be suggested by the teacher if it does not come from the children.

   This circle time follows on from the previous session. Christian Aid produce some excellent resources for primary schools that help the pupils to understand that some children have very different lives from them. The materials contain short narratives describing the lives of children in other countries who do not have the opportunity to attend school, have to do hard manual work to help the family, and who do not have toys, computers, etc. The packs provide the teacher with questions on which to base class discussion. The children are very interested and often shocked at how some children have to live, often prompting a wish to undertake fundraising events.

Links

- PHSE/Cit: Unit 2i, 2j
- SEAL: Relationships
- ECM: Achieve Economic Well-Being
- Geography: Link to the study of countries of the world that experience inequality, such as India, Africa or South America
- RE: Third world charities such as International Aid, Tear Fund, NSPCC, Comic Relief, Children in Need, Cafod, Christian Aid, Barnados, Fair Trade

Theme 2.7 Diversity/respecting differences

Learning objective

To know that different faiths/cultures make up our society.

Reiterate rules

Ask one of the pupils to remind everyone of the circle time roles.

Silent statement

Change places if you enjoy meeting new people.

Question round

At this point the teacher should introduce the visitor and invite them to speak briefly (the teacher and the visitor will obviously have previously agreed on the focus of the visit).

Open round

Invite questions from the children. (They raise their hand to indicate they wish to ask the visitor a question)

Conclusion

Reflect for a minute on what you have heard and then we will finish with a question round. Share with us something you have learned or realised or found interesting.

It is very important to invite visitors into the classroom so that the children can interact with others. The teacher needs to invite people who reflect different background/faiths. There is a wealth of visitors/resources that can be used by the teacher and a series of circle times can be planned to cover this topic.

Visitors can be invited from:

- Local churches, synagogues, mosques, etc.
- Parents/friends from different ethnic backgrounds
- Local charity groups
- Christian Aid
- Barnardos
- NSPCC
- Fair Trade
- International Aid
- Comic Relief
- Children in Need

Many charity/fundraising groups have web sites (see Appendix), leaflets and teaching packs for schools, which can be very useful. Children often become very involved when they are aware of the needs of other groups in society and may like to plan their own fundraising events for these groups. This theme can also be tied into the school assembly.

Links

- PHSE/Cit: Unit 1a, 2i
- SEAL: Relationships
- ECM: Achieve Economic Well-Being
- Geography: Links with units on developing countries
- RE: Units on other faith traditions

Theme 2.8 Multiculturalism

Learning objective

That everyone should understand what is meant by a multicultural society, and how we foster tolerance and respect for each other.

Reiterate rules

Ask one of the pupils to remind everyone of the circle time rules.

Silent statements

Change places if you know anyone who lives in another country.

Change places if you know anyone living in this country who has moved here from another country.

Links

- PHSE/Cit: Units 2a, 2i
- SEAL: Relationships/Getting On and Falling Out
- ECM: Make a Positive Contribution
- Literacy: *Count to Five and Say I'm Alive* book and DVD of poems from a wide variety of cultural backgrounds (available from www.team-video.co.uk)
- Geography: map work, identifying countries on a map
- History: Britain since1930s – Emigration; Invaders and Settlers – Vikings and Romans
- RE: Linked to work on other faith traditions

Question round

Use some initial letter cards and give out one or two letters to each pair in the circle. How many nationalities can they come up with beginning with that letter.

Which food do you like that comes from another country?

Work in pairs. Decide what you think we mean by a multicultural society.

(Teacher may need to help by breaking down the term: multi = ? culture =? society = ?)

Help them to recognise that our country is made up of a mixture of different races all living together.

Open discussion

Why might some people from different ethnic backgrounds be living here?

(Born here, immigration, work, education, holiday, asylum seeking, etc.)

What might they like about being here?

What might they dislike about being here?

What advantages do you think we get from having people from different cultures living with us?

Conclusion

End with a vote to find our favourite foreign foods from among the following:

- spaghetti bolognese
- curry
- Chinese food
- burgers

Theme 2.9 Racism

Learning objective

That everyone understands what we mean by racism and how we foster tolerance and respect for each other.

Reiterate rules

Ask one of the pupils to remind everyone of the circle time rules.

Silent statements

Change places if you have a set of clothes for best/special occasion.

Change places if you have ever been made fun of when you've worn something a bit different.

Question round

Ask the children to name their favourite sports person.

Are all of these sports people from the same race?

In pairs, try to decide what we mean when we talk about a race of people.

(A group of people connected by common origin.)

Open discussion

Why do sports people come here from other countries?

Do you think everyone is happy about this?

Why might they be unhappy? How do you know when they are unhappy?

(Discuss football supporter behaviour – spitting, name calling, etc.)

Why do people react like this?

Does this only happen in sport and to sports people?

How do you think people may feel when they are treated like this?
Share experiences of any racial incidents they have seen or suffered.

This needs to be judged by the teacher and handled sensitively, depending on the class population. The direction the session takes will wholly depend on this.

What is it called when people behave like this and believe their race is better than any other?

Is there anything we can all do to stop racism?

Conclusion

The teacher can find out how to say 'Hello' in several different languages and children can repeat. Teacher can use flash cards and show them the word also. These can also be displayed in classroom:

- French: Salut (silent t)

- German: Guten tag

Links

- PHSE/Cit: Unit 2a, 2c, 2e, 2i
- SEAL: Getting On and Falling Out
- ECM: Make a Positive Contribution
- Music: Listening to music from a variety of cultures, e.g. Reggae, Indian music, Chinese music, Negro spirituals, etc.

- Spanish: Hola (silent h)

- Italian: Ciao (chow)

- Swedish: God dag

- Greek: Yia sou (ya soo)

- Hindi: Na mus thei

- Chinese: Ni hao (nee Ha oh)

- Polish: Dzien dobry

- Croatian: Bok

Alternatively, the children could watch the video from the FA against Racism *Show Racism the Red Card* (Video/DVD with education pack available from www.srtrc.org/resources).

Theme 2.10   The media

Learning objective

To recognise how much our attitudes are influenced by the media.

Reiterate rules

Ask one of the pupils to remind everyone of the circle time rules.

Silent statements

Change places if you have put up your Christmas tree already.

Change places if you have bought any Christmas presents yet.

Question round

What is your favourite thing about Christmas?

What is your least favourite thing about Christmas?

What is your best ever Christmas present?

What is your worst ever Christmas present?

Open discussion

Do you think it's a good thing that so much Christmas advertising begins in the October half term? Do you think people spend too much at Christmas?

Do you think there is too much emphasis on spending? Is this a bad thing? Why? What do you think should happen?

Conclusion

Let's take a vote – Do you think Christmas should by law only begin on December 1st? Think for a few minutes and make sure that you give your own opinion.

Children vote yes, no or abstain.

(Christmas lends itself well to this particular discussion, but staff can adapt it for other occasions/issues, especially where there are children in the class who do not celebrate Christmas.)

Links

- PHSE/Cit: Unit 1a, 2k
- ECM: Make a Positive Contribution
- Literacy: Non-fiction, newspaper reporting
- ICT: Prepare a news report using video equipment announcing that a new law has been passed to stop Christmas advertising until December 1st
- RE: Christmas story
- Art: Christmas art activities

Section 3

Developing a healthy, safer lifestyle

Themes and topics relating to Section 3 of the PHSE/Citizenship scheme of work:

- Healthy eating
- Taking risks
- Keeping safe: Stranger danger
- Keeping safe: Alcohol
- Keeping safe: Smoking
- Hygiene and health
- Health and safety in school

Many topics explored in this section will also be covered in other areas of the curriculum – science, sex and relationships education, PE, etc. This section can be delivered most effectively by inviting a range of visitors to school – the school nurse, a dental hygienist, swimming teachers, fire and police officers, St John's Ambulance personnel, theatre groups, drug education officers and visits from the Life Education Bus (www.lifeeducation.org.uk).

Theme 3.1   Healthy eating

Learning objective

That everyone should be aware that certain foods are better for us than others.

Reiterate rules

Ask one of the pupils to remind everyone of the circle time rules.

Silent statements

Change places if you had breakfast this morning.

Change places if you have a school meal each day.

Change places if you have a packed lunch each day.

Teachers can use any variations of the above statements, and add more in a similar vein.

Question round

What is your favourite food?

What is your least favourite food?

Open discussion

Do you think it is (or would be) a good idea to have only fruit and vegetables for school snack time? Why?

(It should be noted that this is already the case now in many primary schools.)

Can anyone suggest items that we could put into a healthy lunch box? The teacher or a pupil should record suggestions.

Try to ensure that you emphasise that no single food is bad but that our diets need variety – everything in moderation.

Conclusion

Decide on three or four suitable packed lunches. The teacher could ask pupils to record/illustrate for display.

Links

- PHSE/Cit: Unit 3a
- SEAL: Going for Goals
- ECM: Be Healthy
- Science: QCA science units 5A 'Life Cycles' and 5B 'Keeping Healthy'
- Art: Produce either 3D or 2D lunchboxes/plates displaying a healthy meal

Theme 3.2 Taking risks

Links

- PHSE/Cit: Unit 3a, 3e
- SEAL: Going for Goals
- ECM: Stay Safe
- Science: Drug education units
- PE: Outdoor pursuits

Learning objective

That everyone should understand that some risks are worth taking and that we need to be able to decide on which risks are 'good' risks.

Reiterate rules

Ask one of the pupils to remind everyone of the circle time rules.

Silent statements

Change places if you have been to an adventure playground recently.

Change places if you have been swimming and jumped off the diving board.

Teachers can use any variations of the above statements, and add more in a similar vein.

Question round

What do we mean by taking a risk? (Trying out something which may be dangerous.)

Have you ever done anything that you felt scared about but then were really glad you'd done it? Tell us what it was.

Open discussion

Is it good to try out new things? Why/why not? (Suggest some good things to try, e.g. abseiling on an outdoor holiday, and some not so good, e.g. trying a cigarette.)

Do you think people are equally prepared to take risks?

Is it good to be a risk-taker?

Conclusion

Reflection: Just think about yourself for a few minutes – then answer by putting up hands:

I am a risk taker.

OR

I am cautious and don't often take risks.

Theme 3.3 Keeping safe: Stranger danger

Learning objective

That everyone should recognise risk in different situations and make safe choices.

Reiterate rules

Ask one of the pupils to remind everyone of the circle time rules.

Silent statements

Change places if you have ever been persuaded to do something that you know you shouldn't have done?

Change places if you have ever tried to get someone else to do something that they shouldn't do?

Question round

Tell us something that you once did that got you into trouble.

Open discussion

Can anyone think of a situation when it's vitally important to make the right decision so that you don't put yourself in danger?
(Children may offer suggestions about drink, drugs, stranger danger, road safety, smoking, etc.)

1) Give the children this scenario:

    The headteacher tells you in assembly that the police have said that a certain car has been seen hanging around schools when children are going home. They say that everyone must take care and if they see such a car, they must inform an adult – a parent, teacher, after-school club leader, etc.

Why has the head been told to give you this information?

2) Present the children with this problem:

    You are on your way home from the shops and a car slows down beside you. The driver tells you that your Mum has asked them to find you and give you a lift home.

    What do you do?

    Children should know that they say 'No' and find an adult to tell. They should know that things like this may happen at any time or any place, but that the response should always be the same. This needs to be handled sensitively, without the children becoming upset. Try to ensure that they know about safety in numbers – try not to be alone in playgrounds, shops, etc.

Conclusion

Tell pupils that this is not something that happens often. It's very rare, but parents, teachers and police officers have a responsibility to make sure that they know how to handle such a situation correctly in order to keep themselves safe.
    Try the video *What Should I Do?* from Channel 4. This is all about making responsible choices in a variety of situations.

Links

- PHSE/Cit: Unit 3a, 3e
- SEAL: Going for Goals
- ECM: Stay Safe
- Art: Produce a 'Stranger danger' poster

Theme 3.4 Keeping safe: Alcohol

Learning objective

That everyone should recognise risk in different situations and make safe choices.

Reiterate rules

Ask one of the pupils to remind everyone of the circle time rules.

Silent statements

Change places if you have ever been in a pub with an adult.

Change places if you have ever tasted an alcoholic drink.

Question round

Tell us about the occasion when you tasted alcohol and say whether you liked it or not.

This is usually on family occasions – a wedding, Christmas, etc.

Open discussion

Present children with the following scenario:

You go with several friends to one of their houses. Your friend's parents are in a different room from the one where you are all sitting and chatting. Your friend that says there is some wine left in the cupboard and suggests that you all have a drink. What do you do? Discuss the dilemma in pairs and then report back to whole group.

The teacher needs to listen to pupils' ideas and pick up on strategies suggested to make the right/safe decision and handle peer pressure without losing face.

Recap: Why is it not a good idea to drink? What can too much alcohol do to you?

Conclusion

Do you know what a 'teetotaller' is? (Explain if necessary.) Here are some quotes from celebrity teetotallers:

Sadie Frost (designer): 'I've given up drinking . . . I'm looking after my health and feel a million times better.'

Davina McCall (TV presenter): 'I just think I have a better time sober.'

Gwyneth Paltrow (actor): 'I really don't like drunken women; it's such a bad look. I think it's completely inappropriate.'

(Quotes taken from an article in YOU Magazine, 25 March 2007)

Other famous teetotallers include Tom Cruise (actor), Peter Kay (comedian), whose father died of alcoholism, and Chris Martin (lead singer with Coldplay), known for his public disdain of alcohol.

Links

- PHSE/Cit: Unit 3a, 3d, 3f
- SEAL: Going for Goals
- ECM: Be Healthy
- Science: Links to the science units on drug education

Theme 3.5 Keeping safe: Smoking

Learning objective

That everyone should recognise risk in different situations and make safe and effective choices.

Reiterate rules

Ask one of the pupils to remind everyone of the circle time rules.

Silent statement

Change places if you know anyone who smokes.

Question round

Think of some of the places where you have seen people smoking.

Tell us where, and whether the smokers were young or old; male or female.

Open discussion

Why do you think people smoke?

Do you know what it says on packs of cigarettes? (Smoking can kill.)

Do they know what passive smoking is?

The government has now banned smoking in public places. What do you think about this? Why do you think some people feel upset about this?

Present this scenario:
You meet some of your older brother's friends at the shops. They are smoking a cigarette. One of them asks if you have ever smoked and he offers to let you try his cigarette. They all laugh at you when you say no, and they continue to tease you and call you baby names. What do you do? How can you say no successfully?
Discuss in pairs and share your ideas with the group.

Conclusion

Design a poster to show the risks of smoking.

What else could you buy for the same amount?

Teachers could use the same format to discuss other drugs, linked into the pupils' science work, to reiterate the need to think about risk when making choices, so that decisions are informed and safe. There are a range of visitors who can help support the teacher in delivering these topics:

- School nurse
- The police
- Drug education workers
- The Life Bus (www.lifeeducation.org.uk)
- Theatre groups and story tellers.

Links

- PHSE/Cit: Unit 3a, 3d, 3f
- SEAL: Going for Goals
- ECM: Be Healthy
- Maths: Use more calculations for mental starters, e.g. How much per month/year etc?

Theme 3.6 Hygiene and health

Learning objective

To understand that following simple health rules can reduce the spread of germs.

Links

- PHSE/Cit: Unit 3b
- ECM: Be Healthy
- Science: Unit on bacteria

Reiterate rules

Ask one of the pupils to remind everyone of the circle time rules.

Silent statements

Change places if you have been absent this term because of illness.

Change places if you have a handkerchief with you today (not a tissue).

Change places if you have a tissue with you today.

Question round

Think about the last time that you were absent from school because you were ill. What were you suffering from?

Open discussion

Can you remember a time when everyone in your family was suffering from the same illness?

Why do you think everyone became ill at the same time?

Where else might this happen? (School, football matches, restaurants, universities, etc.)

What can we do to help prevent the spread of an illness? (Hand-washing after toilet, before eating, after playtime, etc.; using handkerchiefs, covering mouth when coughing/sneezing; keeping food covered; wiping surfaces, etc.)

How do you think more serious diseases are spread so easily in places such as Africa, India and South America?

Conclusion

Compile a list of rules that can be displayed in the school to remind everyone of good hygiene practice.

The school nurse may come into school and lead a session as a follow-up to this circle time.

A visitor from one of the world charity organisations (or use a video) and you could become involved in fundraising (see Appendix Section 2: Themes 7 and 8).

Theme 3.7 Health and safety in school

This session is useful to deliver if a child in school has a specific medical condition.

Learning objective

To learn how to react in an emergency in school and how and where to get help.

Reiterate rules

Ask one of the pupils to remind everyone of the circle time rules.

Silent statements

Change places if you have ever had an accident in school.

Change places if you have ever helped someone in school who has had an accident.

Question round

In pairs, think of one of our school rules that is there to keep us safe (e.g. not running in corridors, not leaving premises, etc.). Feed back to the circle.

Working with a different partner, discuss what happens when the fire alarm sounds. Feed back to the circle.

Open discussion

Talk about these scenarios:

1) It's a lovely sunny day and everyone is out playing on the field. Suddenly, Tom screams and holds his face. His lip is extremely swollen and red and he says that he has been stung by a wasp. What would you do? (Procedures will vary from school to school, but the teacher needs to inform the children of the correct reaction to each situation.)

2) Everyone is playing on the yard after lunch and Sanjay falls awkwardly during a game of football. He begins to scream in pain and clutches his elbow. He says he can't move his fingers. What would you do?

3) During a lesson, Keshia is excused to go to the toilet. She seems to be taking rather a long time, so the teacher sends you to look for her. When you enter the cloakroom, Sarah says she feels strange and then suddenly she faints, banging her head as she falls. What do you do?

Conclusion

Compile a list for display of guidelines to follow in an emergency situation.

It may be possible to arrange a visit from the St John's Ambulance Service (www.sja.org.uk).

Links

- PSHE/Cit: Unit 3g
- ECM: Be Healthy; Stay Safe
- PE: Safety rules
- DT: Safety rules

Section 4

Developing good relationships and respecting the differences between people

Themes and topics relating to Section 4 of the PHSE/Citizenship scheme of work:

- Friendship
- Reconciliation within friendships
- Resolving conflict
- Bullying (1)
- Bullying (2)
- Disability
- Gender/stereotyping
- Families (1)
- Families (2)
- Families (3)

Theme 4.1 Friendship

Learning objective

That everyone should recognise what makes a good friendship and how to value good friends.

Reiterate rules

Ask one of the pupils to remind everyone of the circle time rules.

Silent statements

Change places if you have one best friend.

Change places if you have lots of different friends.

Question round

Tell us the name of one of your friends and tell us what you like about them.

Open discussion

What qualities would you look for in a friend?

What would it be like if you had no friends? What would you miss?

Conclusion

End with another round after giving time for reflection.

Reflection: 'I think I'm a good friend because ....'

Follow-up ideas:

For display – pupils could make posters saying what makes a good friend, or draw portraits of friends and add captions saying why they like them.

Links

- PHSE/Cit: Unit 1a, 4c
- SEAL: Getting On and Falling Out; Relationships
- ECM: Make a Positive Contribution
- Art: Portraits
- RE: Building Relationships – Biblical friendships – David and Jonathan

Theme 4.2 Reconciliation within friendships

Learning objective

To understand that everyone can disagree and fall out with a friend, but to know how to deal positively with the situation.

Reiterate rules

Ask one of the pupils to remind everyone of the circle time rules.

Links

- PHSE/Cit: Unit 4a, 4c
- SEAL: Getting On and Falling Out; Relationship
- ECM: Make a Positive Contribution
- RE: Christianity Resource Books by Margaret Cooling contain units on reconciliation/friendship

Silent statements

Change places if you have ever fallen out with one of your friends.

Change places if you have ever helped other children to make up after an argument.

Question round

What kind of things do people often fall out about?

How do you feel when you've fallen out with someone?

Open discussion

Present the following scenarios for discussion:

1) A new boy/girl has joined the class and your best friend is now ignoring you and spending time with the new pupil. How do you feel in this situation? How do you deal with it?

Discuss this in pairs and report back to whole group.

2) You tell your best friend a secret and you discover that they have told someone else. How do you feel about this? What should you do?

With another partner, discuss and report back to whole group.
The teacher will make sure that the emotions of jealousy and feeling hurt are covered in the discussions.
Does anyone know what the word reconciliation means?

Conclusion

Apology is often the way to make things better, but it must be genuine. Who finds it difficult to apologise? Take a vote. Why do you think that most people find it so difficult to apologise?

Reflection: Is there anyone you feel you should have apologised to but didn't? Think about how you could put things right while you listen to this music:

'Sorry Seems To Be the Hardest Word' by Elton John

Theme 4.3 Resolving conflict

Learning objective

That everyone should learn the importance of apologising and to be able to accept an apology gracefully and move on.

Reiterate rules

Ask one of the pupils to remind everyone of the circle time rules.

Silent statements

Change places if you have ever accidentally broken something.

Change places if you have accidentally hurt someone in a game.

Links

- PHSE/Cit: Unit 4a, 4d
- SEAL: Getting On and Falling Out; Relationships
- ECM: Make a Positive Contribution
- Literacy: Use as a topic in non-fiction work on discussion texts – presenting both points of view
- Drama: Create short scenarios involving conflict/resolution
- RE: See Christianity Resource Books by Margaret Cooling (as in previous session)

Question round

Has anyone ever taken/broken something belonging to you? Tell us what and how you felt.

Open discussion

Present the following scenarios:

1) In the art lesson, one of your friends accidentally spills paint on a picture that you are really proud of.

How do you feel? How do you think that you would react? What could the friend do to make you feel better?
(Discuss anger, upset, retaliation.)

Do you think that this is a good enough reason to fall out or end the friendship? Why/why not?

2) You are playing football at lunchtime and everyone begins to argue about whether a goal had been scored or not. Eventually, someone lashes out and kicks you because they do not agree with you. Do you kick them back? Why/why not?

Conclusion

Do you find it hard to accept an apology? Having accepted an apology, is there anything else we should do? Suggest strategies for controlling emotions – count to 10, find a 'chill-out' place etc.

Emphasise that the matter should not be mentioned again – let it go – move on.)

Reflection: Think about the good times that you have enjoyed with your friends whilst listening to this music 'You've Got a Friend' by James Taylor.

Theme 4.4 Bullying (1)

Learning objective

That everyone should recognise what we mean by bullying, and identify strategies for dealing with bullying behaviour.

Reiterate rules

Ask one of the pupils to remind everyone of the circle time rules.

Silent statements

Change places if you have ever seen anyone left all alone at playtime.

Change places if you have ever spent playtime alone with no-one to play with.

Question round

Ask the children what they think we mean by bullying.

Open discussion

Present the following scenarios:

1) Someone keeps hiding Asif's belongings. It happens day after day. His bag, pencil case and lunchbox keep being hidden.

Is this bullying? Why/why not? Why might it be happening? What should Stephen do? If he tells the teacher, how do you think they should deal with it?

2) Sanaya always seems to be on her own at playtime with no-one to talk to or play with. She always looks so sad.

Is this bullying? Why/why not? Why might it be happening? Is there anything she can do? Can any adults in school help? How?

Conclusion

As a class, compile a definition of bullying for display, for example:

Bullying is when a person knowingly hurts or intimidates someone else on a regular basis.

Links

- PHSE/Cit: Unit 4a, 4d
- SEAL: Getting On and Falling Out; Relationships
- ECM: Stay Safe; Make a Positive Contribution
- Literacy: There are many books with this theme that could be used as a basis for work in Literacy lessons, e.g. the Harry Potter novels (Dudley and Malfoy), or *Matilda* by Roald Dahl
- Drama: Role, play bullying scenarios, giving a positive ending

Theme 4.5 Bullying (2)

Learning objective

To recognise that bullying doesn't just happen in school.

Reiterate rules

Ask one of the pupils to remind everyone of the circle time rules.

Silent statements

Change places if you have ever seen someone being bullied.

Change places if you have ever been guilty of bullying someone.

Question round

Ask the children if they can think of anywhere that bullying may take place besides school.

(They may suggest places like playgrounds, the baths, parties, at home with siblings, the workplace, etc.)

Open discussion

Present the following scenarios:

1) Kyle goes with a group of friends to the baths. Several of his friends decide to gang up on another child – continually splashing water, bothering them and saying cruel things. They are obviously upset and don't want the attention. Kyle doesn't join in – he just stands and watches, but feels uncomfortable.

Do you think Kyle is guilty of bullying? Why/why not?
Could he have done anything? What?
Who would do nothing?
Who would help the victim?
Who is unsure what they should do?

2) Maria's older brother Ricardo is always on the computer. When Maria asks for her turn, he says he needs it to do homework, although he is always busy playing games. She never gets a turn to use the PC.

Do you think that this is bullying? Why/why not?
Why do you think he is doing this? How do you think Maria may react to this situation? Can she do anything about it? What?
Who would just accept the situation?
Who would argue about it, get angry, tell parents?
Who is not sure what they would do?

Conclusion

Share the words that appear on the following page with the class. They can be used as a poem or turned into a rap. Teachers may have to explain the meaning of some of the words, depending on the age/experience of the children.

Links

- PHSE/Cit: Units 4c, 4a, 4d
- SEAL: Getting On and Falling Out; Relationships
- ECM: Make a Positive Contribution
- Literacy: Extracts from novels, see previous circle time; spelling patterns based on the words on the following page

Bullying

Irritation
Aggravation
Manipulation
Deprivation

Persecution
Execution
Destitution
Retribution

Antagonise
Brutalise
Terrorise
Monopolise

Aggression
Possession
Oppression
Depression

Scattered
Battered
Tattered
Shattered.

Viv Smith

Theme 4.6 Disability

Learning objective

To heighten awareness of disabilities, to foster respect and to value everyone's contribution to society.

(**Note**: teachers will need to prepare a range of pictures from magazines or newspapers of different people – see below.)

Reiterate rules

Ask one of the pupils to remind everyone of the circle time rules.

Silent statements

Change places if you have blue eyes.

Change places if you have blonde hair.

Change places is you are small for your age.

Change places if you are tall for your age.

Change places if you are right-handed.

Change places if you wear glasses.

Question round

What do you think the word disability means?

Allow the children to discuss with a partner and then report back.

Ensure that the children understand the range of disabilities in society – visual or hearing impairment, physical difficulty, speech problems, mental problems, diabetes, epilepsy, ADHD, OCD, depression, etc.

Show the children a selection of portraits. (Images can be collected from newspapers, magazines, etc.) They should show young and old, male and female individuals. Suggest a range of disabilities as described above and see if pupils can match the picture with the disability. Establish that we cannot always tell that people may have difficulties just by appearance.

Open discussion

What causes people to be disabled (congenital problems, genetic reasons, an accident or illness)?

Can you think of anything that we can do to make things easier for people who have a disability?

Children can discuss ramps, hearing loops, signing, flashing phones, dogs, toilet facilities, transport modification, riding for the disabled, etc.

Do you think that it's important to help as much as we can?
Do we do enough?

Has anyone ever watched the paralympics? Show the children pictures of Tanni Gray Thompson. Has anyone heard of Tanni? Do you know what has she achieved? Give a short synopsis. Teachers can find images and information on internet on Tanni's own web site (www.tanni.co.uk).

Links

- PHSE/Cit: Unit 4a, 4f
- SEAL: Its Good to be Me
- ECM: Stay Safe, Make a Positive Contribution
- Literacy: Write a biography of a high profile personality who has a disability – e.g. Tanni Grey Thompson, David Blunkett, Heather Mills, Evelyn Glennie, etc.
- Use the novels – *Sticky Beak* and *Blabber Mouth* by Morris Gleitzman, which have a deaf heroine
- ICT: Use to research the biographies

Conclusion

Does anyone have a friend, relative or acquaintance who has a disability?

Children can show by raising their hands. Does anyone know the symbol for disability access? Show this image.

There are a range of visitors who may be happy to come into school and talk to the children to support this topic:

* A signer

* A parent/friend who uses a wheelchair

* A representative from Guide Dogs for the Blind

* Someone from Society for the Blind, who will show the children some for the aids to help someone who is visually impaired

* A representative of Help the Aged.

Theme 4.7 Gender/stereotyping

This could be used to introduce discussions about human sexuality (if the teacher feels that this is appropriate for their class group).

Learning objective

To recognise what is meant by 'stereotyping' and the importance of challenging stereotyping.

(**Note**: The definition will be addressed during the session – don't give it now as it may influence the children's answers.)

Reiterate rules

Ask one of the pupils to remind everyone of the circle time rules.

Silent statements

Change places if you are a girl.

Change places if you are a boy.

Change places if you have a good friend who is of the opposite sex to you.

Question round

Something I think that is good about being a girl/boy is ....

Do you have an interest hobby that people normally associate with the opposite sex to you? Tell us about it.

Open discussion

Show the children a picture of a woman. In pairs, the children should suggest a job they may do. (The teacher scribes results.)

Repeat the activity with the picture of a man.

The teacher should then read out the lists. The expectation here is that they will be stereotyped lists, i.e. the woman would be a nurse, secretary, teacher or hairdresser, and the man would be a doctor, engineer, scientist, footballer or soldier.

What do you notice about the two lists? Are there any jobs now that women can do that they didn't do before? What about the men?

Do you think this is good? Why/why not?

Show the children a series of pictures that they can collect from newspapers, magazines, etc. – a vagrant, a punk, a black person, a teenager, an OAP, a girl, a boy, etc.

Which one of these people do you think stole an old lady's bag?

Which one do you think begs on the street?

Which one do you think has been mugged?

Which one do you think has got off the bus without paying?

The teacher may use his/her own questions. Why did you choose the answers that you gave?

Links

- PHSE/Cit: Unit 4a, 4e, 4f
- SEAL: It's Good to be Me
- ECM: Stay Safe; Make a Positive Contribution
- Literacy: *Bill's New Frock* by Ann Fine
- History: Britain in World War 2 – Women undertaking male jobs

Has anyone ever heard the word 'stereotype'? Does anyone know what it means?

Explain that it is making a judgement about someone based on their appearance without knowing them or knowing anything about them. The teacher can remind the children of the saying 'Don't judge a book by its cover').

Conclusion

Finish with a round –

What do you think you may like to do when you leave school?

Theme 4.8 Families (1)

Learning objective

To develop an understanding of what families are and that all family units are not the same.

Reiterate rules

Ask one of the pupils to remind everyone of the circle time rules.

Silent statements

Change places if there are three people or less living in your family home.

Change places if there are more than three people living in your family home.

Change places if your grandma or granddad lives with you.

Question round

Have you noticed any differences between your family and your friends' families. What are they?

Open discussion

What do you think a family is? Is it always a child's parents who lives with them and cares for them?

What do you think are the most important things about a family (love, respect, loyalty, care, security, support, sharing)?

As a class, produce an acrostic poem based on the word 'family' to display in the classroom.

This can be a very sensitive issue, as family groups are very diverse and children's experiences are very different. The topic will need sensitive handling from the teacher, who may wish to adjust these questions, depending on the class group.

Conclusion

Give the children five minutes to quickly sketch their own family group in silence as 'We Are Family' by Sister Sledge is played (all adults present should also participate). The teacher will then say '1 . . . 2 . . . 3 . . . Show'. All will hold up their family pictures to share with everyone.

Display pictures along with the class poem.

Change places if you and your family were born in Britain but you have a lot of relatives who still live in another country.

Links

- PHSE/Cit: Unit 4a, 4c, 1d
- SEAL: It's Good to be Me
- ECM: Make a Positive Contribution
- Art: Portraits/figure drawing
- RE: Christian Resource Books by Margaret Cooling; Unit on families
- Visitor: Representative from Banardos

Theme 4.9 Families (2)

Learning objective

To understand what families expect of each other and members' individual responsibility within the family.

Reiterate rules

Ask one of the pupils to remind everyone of the circle time rules.

Silent statements

Change places if you have had an argument with a family member in the last few days.

Change places if you have spent some time chatting to a family member recently.

Question round

Tell us about something that you have done this week to help a member of your family.

Tell us what you do as a family that you really enjoy.

Open discussion

Present these short scenarios:

1) You want to walk on your own one evening to visit a friend's house. It is several streets away from where you live. Your parents say no.

Is this fair? Why/why not?
Why might your parents have said no? Can you think of a solution to the problem?
Try to develop the idea of compromise (e.g. they could walk there and their parents pick them up, or they could walk and meet friend half way, etc.).

2) Tao and Yuan are brother and sister. Although Tao is 10 and Yuan is 8, their parents always decide that they should go to bed at the same time each night.

Is this fair? Why/why not? Why do you think the parents do this? Can you think of a solution to this problem?

Conclusion

Take suggestions from the children as to how they can demonstrate care for other members of their family, for example by keeping their room tidy, not arguing when asked to do a chore, trying not to squabble, etc.

Reflect on the suggestions and choose one that they could aim to do more regularly within their family.

The most appropriate of these could be added to the display from last circle time, along with any photos from home.

Links

*   PHSE/Cit: Unit 4a, 4c, 1d
*   SEAL: Getting On and Falling Out; Relationships
*   ECM: Make a Positive Contribution
*   Art: Bring in photos from home and use to produce portraits
*   Literacy: Compose a class acrostic poem using the word COMPROMISE
*   RE: Caring for others

Theme 4.10 Families (3)

Learning objective

To understand that feeling jealous is a common emotion and to develop strategies to cope with sibling rivalry.

Reiterate rules

Ask one of the pupils to remind everyone of the circle time rules.

Silent statements

Change places if you are an only child.

Change places if you have a brother or sister.

Change places if your brother or sister is younger than you.

Links

- PHSE/Cit: Unit 4a, 4c, 1d
- SEAL: Good to be Me; Relationships
- ECM: Make a Positive Contribution
- Art: What colour do the children associate with jealousy? Use an abstract painting that signifies the emotion of jealousy as a stimulus
- RE: The Ten Commandments; there are many stories from all major faiths using jealousy as a theme – e.g. Rama and Sita

Question round

Can anyone explain what it means to be jealous (wanting something someone else has)?

Have you ever felt jealous of someone (a friend or family member)? Can you tell us who and why?

How does jealousy make you feel?

Open discussion

Why do you think that people feel jealous? Have you ever heard the term 'sibling rivalry'? Can anyone explain what it means?

    Has anyone experienced having a new baby in the house? How does it make you feel?

(Responses may be either positive or negative – if only one of these is offered, the teacher should put the opposite side. Explore why people may feel like they do.)

If you ever feel hurt or angry because you are jealous, can you think of things which may make you feel better?

(You can apologise to your friend/sibling if you've been unkind, you can talk feeling through with an adult, you can do something you enjoy to take your mind off problem and make you feel better, etc.)

Conclusion

I don't need to feel jealous because......... Each child makes a positive statement about anything from their life.

Section 5

Assessment, recording and reporting

In this section, we have offered some suggestions to teachers for assessing pupils in PHSE/ Citizensip. We have included some simple proformas that you may wish to photocopy and use to record their observations.

Assessment, recording and reporting

Assessing children during practical activities is always a difficult task for teachers, and circle time is no exception. By its very nature, circle time, once it is underway, is a continuous process with no time for the teacher to make formal notes and, indeed, it would not be appropriate for the teacher to be seen by the children to be assessing their responses.

We believe that recording and assessment should be meaningful, but not be an onerous task for busy primary school teachers. Monitoring and assessing attainment of pupils in PSHE/Citizenship can seem difficult, however there are often important insights to be noted during the sessions, which can be of great value to the teacher at a later date. Also, it can be encouraging to see how certain children's responses and attitudes have changed and/or improved throughout the year.

For this reason, an assessment sheet has been included that can be completed by the teacher at the end of each session or at the end of a series of circle times. It is quite an open sheet and is mainly for the teacher to make short notes on any children they feel have made exceptional contributions to the session by way of their responses; children whose responses they feel have improved; children who have taken little or no part in the session; and children they have particular concerns about.

Good responses may show that a child has a real awareness of the subject being discussed; answers questions thoughtfully; responds to another child's comments in a constructive way; demonstrates eagerness to express their opinions and present logical arguments; and shows understanding of an issue and its implication for the wider community.

Improved responses may show that a child 'passes' less frequently; has begun to express their own opinions rather than copying other's responses; behaves in a more appropriate way during the sessions; is seen to be making a greater contribution during the sessions; or is beginning to express themselves more clearly and with a more varied vocabulary.

Poor responses may show that a child 'passes' on every occasion; appears to have no opinions of their own or to copy others' responses; never offers answers to questions; is disruptive; and appears not to be listening or concentrating, with any answers given being very simplistic or repetitive.

Concerns may alert the teacher to a child becoming withdrawn; having poor self-esteem; having an inappropriate attitude to certain subjects; having an inability to concentrate for even short periods; or giving negative responses.

An end-of-year assessment sheet has also been included, which can be used to quickly assess each child's response to circle time sessions. This could be in the form of either just a tick or accompanied by additional comments.

Circle time assessments can be very useful when completing end-of-year reports to parents as they can contribute to PSHE/Citizenship, Speaking and Listening and a child's personal statement.

Recording

A simple recording sheet has been included that will assist the teacher in monitoring which sections have been covered during the term and subsequently the year. This will show at a glance which themes still need to be addressed before the end of the year.

Session Assessment Sheet

Circle Time Theme:

Date:

Good Responses:

Improved Responses:

Poor Responses

Any Concerns:

End-of-section Recording Sheet

This sheet presents an overview of topics addressed throughout the year and acts as a running record for the teacher to help plan topics still needing to be covered.

Section 1: Developing confidence and responsibility and making the most of your abilities

Theme	Date
The new school year	
Self-esteem	
Emotions: Anger	
Emotions: Disappointment	
Emotions: Excitement	
Adult roles	
School transfer	
Handling money	
Bereavement: Pets	
Bereavement: Family	

Section 2: Preparing to play an active role as citizens

Theme	Date
Rules	
Classroom rules	
Rights and responsibilities	
Democracy	
Prejudice	
Inequality	
Diversity/respecting differences	
Multiculturalism	
Racism	
The media	

Using Circle Time for PHSE and Citizenship © Daphne Gutterigde and Viv Smith, Routledge, 2008

Section 3: Developing a healthy, safer lifestyle

Theme	Date
Healthy eating	
Taking risks	
Keeping safe: Stranger danger	
Keeping safe: Alcohol	
Keeping safe: Smoking	
Hygiene and health	
Health and safety in school	

Section 4: Developing good relationships and respecting the differences between people

Theme	Date
Friendship	
Reconciliation within friendships	
Resolving conflict	
Bullying (1)	
Bullying (2)	
Disability	
Gender/stereotyping	
Families (1)	
Families (2)	
Families (3)	

End-of-year Assessment Sheet

Name	Good responses	Improved responses	Poor responses	Concerns

Appendix

Useful resources
for teachers

Useful web sites, books, music and art resources have been listed in this appendix in section order.

Section 1 Developing confidence and responsibility and making the most of your abilities

1.2 Self-esteem

Books: Harry Potter Series by J K Rowling
Music: 'What Have You Done Today To Make You Feel Proud?' by M People

1.3 Emotions: Anger

Music: 'Mars' from *The Planet Suite* by Gustav Holst
Art: Any piece by Jackson Pollack

1.5 Emotions: Excitement

Music: 'I Feel So Excited' by The Pointer Sisters
        The theme from 'Fame' by Irene Cara
Art: Any piece by Mondrian

1.7 School transfer

Web site: 'Moving On' game from Lancashire Healthy Schools Team, available from www.lancsngfl.ac.uk

1.10 Bereavement: Family

Music: 'Father and Son' by Cat Stevens
Books: *Grandpa* by John Burningham
        Beautiful by Susi Fowler
        Michael Rosen's Sad Book by Michael Rosen
        Vicky Angel by Jacqueline Wilson

Section 2 Preparing to play an active role as citizens

2.1 Rules

Book: *Matilda* by Roald Dahl

2.3 Rights and responsibilities

Books: *Oliver Twist* by Charles Dickens
Water Babies by Charles Kingsley
The Street Child by Berlie Doherty

Web sites: United Nations Children's Charter www.childrens-charterofrights.com/poster1;
www.qca.org.uk

2.4 Democracy

Web sites: www.schoolcoucils.org
www.savethechildren.org.uk
www.localdemocracy.org.uk
www.bys.org.uk
www.teachingcitizenship.org.uk
www.dfes.gov.uk/citizenship
www.mockelections.co.uk
DVD: *The X File*, available from www.channel4learning.net/support/programmenotes/
citizenship

2.5 Prejudice

Books: *Diary of Anne Frank*
Rose Blanche by Roberto Innocenti
Coming Home by Floella Benjamin

2.6 Inequality

and

2.7 Diversity/respecting differences

Web sites: www.live8live.com
www.fairtrade.org.uk
www.christianaid.com
www.internationalaid.com
www.comicrelief.com
www.cafod.org.uk
www.barnados.org.uk
www.nspcc.co.uk
www.tearfund.org

2.8 Multiculturalism

Book/DVD: *Count to Five and Say I'm Alive*, available from www.team-video.co.uk

2.9 Racism

DVD/Education Pack: *Show Racism the Red Card*, available from www.srtrc.org/resources
www.theredcard.ie/news

Section 3 Developing a healthy, safer lifestyle

3.1 Healthy eating

DVD: Health Education Collection 44320, available from www.4learningshop.co.uk

3.4 Keeping safe: Alcohol

Web site: www.wiredforhealth.gov.uk

3.5 Keeping safe: Smoking

DVD: *What Should I Do?* PSHE and Citizenship Collection 44323, available from www.4learningshop.co.uk
Web sites: Life Education www.lifeeducation.org.uk
        Drug Education Packs www.scotland.gov.uk/publications

3.7 Health and safety in school

Web site: www.sja.org.uk

Section 4 Developing good relationships and respecting the differences between people

4.2 Reconcilliation within friendships

Books: Christianity Topic Books 1, 2, 3 by Margaret Cooling
Music: 'Sorry Seems To Be The Hardest Word' by Elton John

4.3 Resolving conflict

Music: 'You've Got a Friend' by James Taylor

4.4 Bullying (1)

4.5 Bullying (2)

Books: Harry Potter Series by J K Rowling
           Matilda by Roald Dahl
Web sites: www.dfes.gov.uk/bullying (video/DVD also available)
           www.childline.org.uk/bullying
           www.bullying.co.uk
           www.bullyonline.org/
           www.nspcc.org.uk

4.6 Disability

Web site: www.tanni.com.uk
DVD: *Being Different/That's My Life* 443428 available from www.4learningshop.co.uk
Books: *Sticky Beak/Blabber Mouth* by Morris Gleitzman

4.7 Gender/stereotyping

Book: *Bill's New Frock* by Ann Fine

4.8 Families (1)

Music: 'We Are Family' by Sister Sledge